A Robbie Reader

Gardening For Kids

Design Your Own Pond and Water Garden

Susan Sales Harkins and William H. Harkins

Mitchell Lane
PUBLISHERS

P.O. Box 196
Hockessin, Delaware 19707
Visit us on the web: www.mitchelllane.com
Comments? email us: mitchelllane@mitchelllane.com

Gardening For Kids

A Backyard Flower Garden for Kids

A Backyard Vegetable Garden for Kids

Design Your Own Butterfly Garden

Design Your Own Pond and Water Garden

A Kid's Guide to Landscape Design

A Kid's Guide to Perennial Gardens

ABOUT THE AUTHORS: Susan and Bill Harkins live in Kentucky and they enjoy writing together for children. Susan has written many books for adults and children. Bill is a history buff and helps Kentuckians prepare for earthquakes and other natural disasters as a member of the Civil Air Patrol. Bill and Susan both share a love for gardening and have nurtured several flower gardens and ponds.

PUBLISHER'S NOTE: The facts on which the story in this book is based have been thoroughly researched. Documentation of such research can be found on page 46. While every possible effort has been made to ensure accuracy, the publisher will not assume liability for damages caused by inaccuracies in the data, and makes no warranty on the accuracy of the information contained herein.

Library of Congress Cataloging-in-Publication Data

Harkins, Susan Sales.
  Design your own pond and water garden / by Susan Sales Harkins and William H. Harkins.
      p. cm.—(Robbie reader. Gardening for kids)
  Includes bibliographical references and index.
  ISBN 978-1-58415-635-2 (library bound)
  1. Water gardens—Juvenile literature. 2. Ponds—Juvenile literature. I. Harkins, William H. II. Title. III. Series.
  SB423.H37 2008
  635.9'674—dc22
                                        2008002256

Printing 1 2 3 4 5 6 7 8 9

                                                      PLB

Contents

Introduction 4

Chapter One
Designing a Backyard Water Garden 7

Chapter Two
Digging, Lining, and Finishing Touches 13

Chapter Three
Choosing and Caring for Water Plants 21

Chapter Four
Choosing Fish and Other Livestock 29

Chapter Five
Maintenance and Troubleshooting 37

Craft Toad House 42

Appendix 1 Math Formulas 44

Appendix 2 Planting Water Lilies 45

Further Reading 46

    Books 46

    Works Consulted 46

    Internet 46

Glossary 47

Index 48

Words in **bold** type can be found in the glossary.

Introduction

A garden is as unique as its maker, and that's what makes creating one so exciting. Enjoying the garden is certainly a good goal, but gardening is an ongoing adventure that begins with a simple idea. First, you plan. Then you measure, dig, plant, weed, and water. Being outdoors and close to the warm soil can enrich your life.

When you're not on your knees tending and nurturing, sit back and enjoy the life your garden attracts. A trickling waterfall bubbles and gurgles and brings beautiful songbirds to your yard. Butterflies and dragonflies skip from bloom to bloom.

Hummingbirds dance in the treetops. One buzzes close to your head. Be careful not to swat at it! A sea of reds, yellows, blues, oranges—every color in the rainbow—is right at your fingertips. Close your eyes and touch the velvety petals or enjoy the sweet and spicy scents.

Gardening brings the best nature has to offer to your own backyard, whether you live near the beach, in the mountains, on the plains, or in a city. With a little imagination, you can add beauty and life to your own yard.

Chapter

1

Designing a Backyard Water Garden

Almost everyone enjoys sitting on a riverbank or relaxing near a pond. The air near any body of water is refreshing and gentle. You can add peacefulness and beauty to your yard by creating a small water garden. It will entertain you while providing a stable **ecosystem** for plant and fish life. Your pond's health depends on sunshine, plants, and the right amount of water.

Where you put your pond is the most important decision you'll make. Keep the following things in mind while searching for the perfect spot:

* **Always get your parents' permission before digging in the yard.**
* Have your parents check with gas, electric, phone, and cable services for the location and depth of underground lines.
* Your pond needs at least five hours of sunlight a day.
* Decide whether you want to see the pond from inside your home.
* The spot should be mostly flat.
* Rocky or hard ground is hard to dig.
* Don't put your pond near trees, or you'll spend a lot of time removing leaves.

* Avoid a spot that floods or where rainwater **surges**.
* Don't put your pond in a **bog** or waterlogged spot. Water pressure from below the surface might damage it.

Try to pick the sunniest spot in your yard. However, a pond that is always in the bright sunshine will quickly turn green with tiny plant life called **algae** (AL-jee). That's why water plants are so important. Water lilies unroll their leaves across the surface of the water, blocking the sunlight, which starves algae.

Make sure you can get to and into the pond easily for cleanup, repairs, and maintenance. At first, you'll need a hose to fill the pond. Later, you'll need it for cleanup and to top off the pond once in a while.

Pond Tip

*Your fish won't freeze during the winter in a shallow pond. **Toxic** gases under the ice, and not the cold, kills fish. Fish breathe in oxygen and breathe out carbon dioxide. Normally, carbon dioxide escapes through the surface. In the winter, ice can trap gases and poison the fish. Cut a hole about six to eight inches in diameter through the ice so that gases can escape. Don't use an ice pick or other sharp tool. Instead, set an empty metal can (a coffee can works fine) on the ice and have **an adult** fill it with boiling water. Or insert a special heating element made for ponds before it freezes.*

A waterfall adds movement and sound to your yard. The noise from a gentle waterfall will attract songbirds. Don't be surprised if you see small birds drinking from and bathing in your waterfall!

A waterfall needs an electric pump, which you will need to plug in. Install your pond close to an electrical outlet. Running an extension cord across the lawn is a bad idea. Someone might trip over it. Even worse, if you forget to remove it while mowing the grass, a lawn mower blade might slice it and **electrocute** (ee-LEK-troh-kyoot) someone. Your pond doesn't have to have a waterfall, but the fish will like it.

Your pond's size depends on the size of your yard. You'll need at least 50 square feet of surface area. That only sounds big. A seven-foot square, or a five-foot by ten-foot rectangle, or an eight-foot

When purchasing fish, ask lots of questions. Koi (pictured) are colorful fish, but they are expensive and hard to keep. Goldfish add a splash of brilliant color and are easy to raise.

circle are all about 50 square feet. (See Appendix 1, page 44, for figuring surface area.) Your pond can be much bigger, but it shouldn't be smaller.

The least important design element is shape. You won't benefit much from the pond's shape because you won't view it from overhead. You'll glance across your yard at it. Don't create small streams and runs. You won't be able to maintain their natural balance. Simple designs with gentle curves are best because they're easy to dig, build, and maintain.

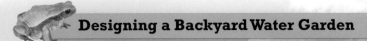

It's hard to move a pond! Spend a lot of time walking your yard. Notice how much sun different areas get during the day. Take notes and make sketches as you go.

A shallow pond can support plant and fish life— if you choose the right plants and fish. Fifteen inches is deep enough for most hardy water lilies, but twenty-four inches is best for fish. Vertical sides might seem like a good idea, but they're hard to build and might collapse under stress. A steep slope of about 70 degrees (20 degrees less than straight up and down) is best.

The ideal pond supports plants and fish with little maintenance. It has the proper balance of sunshine, plants, and water volume. Plan a pond with at least 50 square feet of surface area and sides that slope quickly to a depth of 24 inches.

Digging, Lining, and Finishing Touches

Coming up with a design that focuses on plants and fish is the first step to creating a water garden. The next step is to decide what to use to line your pond. The three most common materials are concrete, sheet liners, and preformed molds.

A concrete pond is strong, but concrete is expensive and doesn't bend. As the water freezes in the winter, the ice can cause cracks. If you're set on concrete, ask your parents if they can hire a professional. Don't let anyone talk you into gently sloping sides. Sloping sides are easier to build, but your pond won't hold as much water. Fill and drain the cured concrete pond several times during the first six weeks to remove lime from the new concrete. Lime will kill plants and fish. If you're in a hurry, paint the concrete with a special sealant.

Another expensive material is sheet lining. It's durable, easy to install and repair, and flexible. However, all liners aren't created equal. Butyl (BYOO-til) rubber is the most expensive but also the most durable sheet liner. It's the least likely to tear or puncture and could last up to fifty years. Polyvinyl chloride (PAH-lee-VY-nil KLOR-yd) or PVC is less expensive than butyl rubber. It is

more likely to puncture, but it's easy to repair. This liner might last up to fifteen years. Polythene (PAH-lee-theen) is the least expensive of the sheet liners, but direct sunlight damages it. Even properly protected, this liner will last only a few years. Use black, 1,000-gauge (thickness) sheets to get the best wear. Cover the edges above the water level with decorative rocks to protect it from sun damage.

To figure out how much sheet lining you need, mark off a rectangle large enough to fit the pond. Then, add twice the depth to both the length and width. For instance, a free-form shape that fits into a 13-by-11-foot rectangle and has a depth of 2 feet needs a liner that is (13 + 2 + 2) by (11 + 2 + 2), which equals 17 by 15 feet (see diagram). If you use polythene, add about an extra foot to both

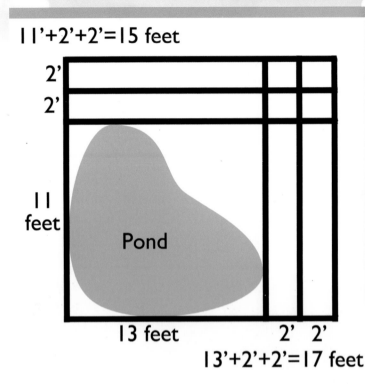

11'+2'+2'=15 feet

2'

2'

11 feet

Pond

13 feet

2' 2'

13'+2'+2'=17 feet

This odd-shaped pond fits into a rectangle that is 13 feet by 11 feet. To figure the size of the liner you'll need, add twice the depth (2 x 2 ft) to both the length (13 ft) and width (11 ft). The liner will need to be 17 ft x 15 ft.

length and width for edging, because it doesn't stretch as well as the other two types.

To install, dig the hole a few inches deeper than the pond's deepest point. Use a level to make sure the bottom and edges are balanced from side to side. Don't skip this step. A lopsided pond looks terrible. Check the ground for sharp rocks. Using a board or a shovel, press the edges and bottom to **compact** the dirt as much as possible. Line the bottom and sides with a soft material such as newspaper, old carpeting, or pond matting.

Once you decide where your pond will go and what it will look like, you can start digging. This step can be even more fun if you invite some friends to help.

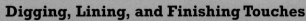

Many large ponds have shelves for plants that require different planting depths. A depth of two feet is good for most backyard ponds.

Lay the liner over the cushion layer. Pull the edges up over the sides and anchor them with rocks or bricks. Turn on the water to fill the hole. The weight of the water will stretch the liner into the shape. Smooth out wrinkles as you find them.

Preformed liners are hard molded plastic that come in many shapes and sizes. To install, turn the form upside

Pond Tip

Check the weather forecast before digging your pond. You want a dry day. Plan to start and finish the project in the same day if possible. You might have to reshape and tamp down the sides and bottom of your hole if it rains before you get your lining material in place.

Preformed liners are easy to install and maintain. Use the outer shelf for water plants that like shallow water.

down and, on the ground, mark a rectangle or square large enough for the form. Using the rectangle as a guide, dig the hole as deep as the pond's deepest part. Use a level to make sure the hole is balanced from side to side. Then, place the mold in the hole. Fill in the hole around the form using soil or sand. Continue to use the level as you fill this in and make adjustments. Add water and allow it to settle for a few days.

Underwater lights are a nice touch, but you don't need expensive **submersible** (sub-MER-suh-bul) ones. A few solar lights around the edge of your pond will do. They're inexpensive, easy to install, and require no electricity.

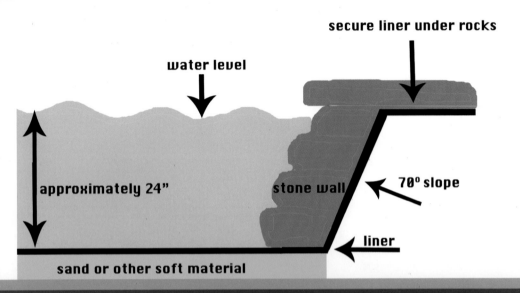

secure liner under rocks

water level

approximately 24"

stone wall

70° slope

liner

sand or other soft material

Follow these general guidelines for balance: Your pond should be 18 to 24 inches deep—although in colder parts of the country, 36 inches is recommended. Slope the sides at 70 degrees, and extend a few flat rocks over the water's edge to provide a hiding place for fish.

No matter what material you use for a lining, you'll need to finish the edges. Cover them with rocks, paving stones, or even bricks. Position flat rocks over the inside edge of your pond. The overlap will give your fish an extra place to hide.

Use tap water to fill your pond. Don't use water from a pond or lake. You might accidentally transfer pollution or harmful life-forms into your pond.

Choosing and Caring for Water Plants

Water plants are essential, but that doesn't mean they can't be beautiful. Water lilies provide both beauty and balance. Their spreading leaves shade the water from sunlight, which keeps the water clear. Below the surface, **oxygenators** (OK-seh-jeh-nay-turs) keep the pond healthy. Plant tall grasses along the edge to give the pond a natural look.

By far, water lilies are the most important plant for your water garden. Most hardy lilies grow well throughout the United States. They are easy to keep, and they grow year round in warm climates. In colder regions, they'll flower from June to October.

Most lilies need a planting depth of 10 to 16 inches. For water plants, the term *planting depth* refers to the amount of water between the top of the plant's soil and the surface of the water. *Soil depth* is the amount of soil needed to **nourish** the plant. For instance, the red *Pygmaea rubra* needs a 3- to 9-inch planting depth and 5 inches of

Instead of water lilies, water hyacinths (HY-uh-sinths) may be placed in your pond to give it shade.

soil (see Appendix 2 on page 45 for recommended planting and soil depths).

Use upside-down plant containers, bricks, or flat stones to build a platform of just the right height for each lily. For instance, in a 24-inch-deep pond, you'd need a platform of 10 to 16 inches high for a *Pygmaea rubra.* Use this formula for figuring out platform height:

pond depth – (soil depth + planting depth) = height of planting platform

Platform materials must be safe for plants and fish. Never use cement blocks unless you treat them with a sealant. Use materials that have no sharp or rough edges.

For the best balance, you'll want to cover about two-thirds of the water's surface with plant life. If you are using lilies, think about how much of the surface each lily will cover. Use this formula to figure out how many plants of the same kind you'd need:

(pond's square footage ÷ 2/3) ÷ plant's surface coverage = number of plants

You would need about 26 *Pygmaea rubra* to cover two-thirds of a 50-square-foot pond (about 32 square feet). To make a more natural garden, choose lilies of different kinds. To figure out which kind and how many of each, check with a local plant nursery to see what's available and what would do well in a pond that is the depth of yours. Add up the coverage of each type until you reach two-thirds of the pond's surface.

Pond Tip

If you use a sheet liner, buy extra and place small sheets of it under each plant platform to protect the actual liner. Simply cut a piece a little larger than the platform's base. The extra layer will protect the main lining from sharp points and rough edges. Check the protective pieces regularly for wear and tear, and replace them when needed. If you wade into your pond, go barefoot or wear rubber flip-flops to avoid tearing the liner.

For example, you might use the following mix for a 50-square-foot pond:

2	*Odorata rosea* (pink)	10 square feet
1	*Tuberosa richardsoni* (white)	8 square feet
3	*Laydekeri fulgens* (red)	9 square feet
4	*Pygmaea helvola* (yellow)	5 square feet

The total square footage of this mix is 32, which is about two-thirds of the pond's surface. The mix includes different colors and sizes.

Before you buy, examine all your plants carefully for snails, beetles, grubs, and egg clusters. Don't forget the underside of each leaf—that's where you'll find most eggs. However, do not use **pesticides** (PES-tih-syds) on your lilies. Pesticides, meant to kill insect pests, will also kill fish.

Lilies need heavy, rich garden soil. Fertilizer will make algae grow, so don't use it. It's best if your lilies get **nutrients** (NOO-tree-unts) from their soil rather than from fertilizer. You don't have to, but you might want to repot new lilies so that you can control the soil's quality and depth.

After a few years' growth, you will have to repot your plants in larger pots so that their roots have plenty of room to grow. If you have to repot a lily, lay the **rhizome** (RY-zohm) flat across the top of fresh soil, about an inch below the top of the pot. Cover with soil until just the growing tip is showing. Pack the soil firmly, and cover the soil with a shallow layer of gravel or pebbles. Use a larger rock to anchor the pot in place. Within two weeks, stems and leaves will grow. Lilies prefer still water, so don't place them near currents created by filters and pumps.

Oxygenators are small plants that live below the

A variety of plants, such as water-hugging lilies mixed with tall grasses, will make your pond more interesting.

Pond Tip

*If your fish breed and you want the eggs to hatch, move the eggs to an aquarium. Otherwise, fish and other visitors to your pond will eat them. Hatching fish eggs isn't hard, but it does take a bit of know-how. Don't be discouraged if you don't succeed right away. Buy a book on fish or check one out from your library and keep trying. Don't move **fry** back to the pond until they're big enough to survive. Fish and pond visitors eat fry.*

water's surface and produce oxygen. It does not matter which kinds you choose because you won't see them. Even without them, your fish will get enough oxygen through the water's surface. The benefit of oxygenators is that they compete with algae for food. For ponds smaller than 100 square feet, plant one bunch for every two square feet of water surface. (For a 50-square-foot pond, you'll need 25 bunches.) Drop them in and hope for the best, or anchor the roots near bricks, pebbles, or rocks for faster growth.

Marginal (MAR-jih-nul) plants grow along the shoreline in shallow water. Most are tall grasses and reed-type plants. They are strictly for looks because they add nothing to the pond's balance. Marginals look best when planted in groups. Some plants will take over a spot if you let them. They send out shoots that invade other pots and choke out the original plant. You can keep these fast-growing plants under control by placing a brick or stone between pots.

Line the edge of your pond with marginals. They'll provide a natural-looking border while hiding the pond's lining. Your fish might even turn that area into a nursery.

Doing so blocks the shoots. When you see shoots, simply break them off and throw them away.

Plant all of your aquatic plants while they are actively growing. In colder regions, plant from May through September. In warmer climates, you can plant anytime.

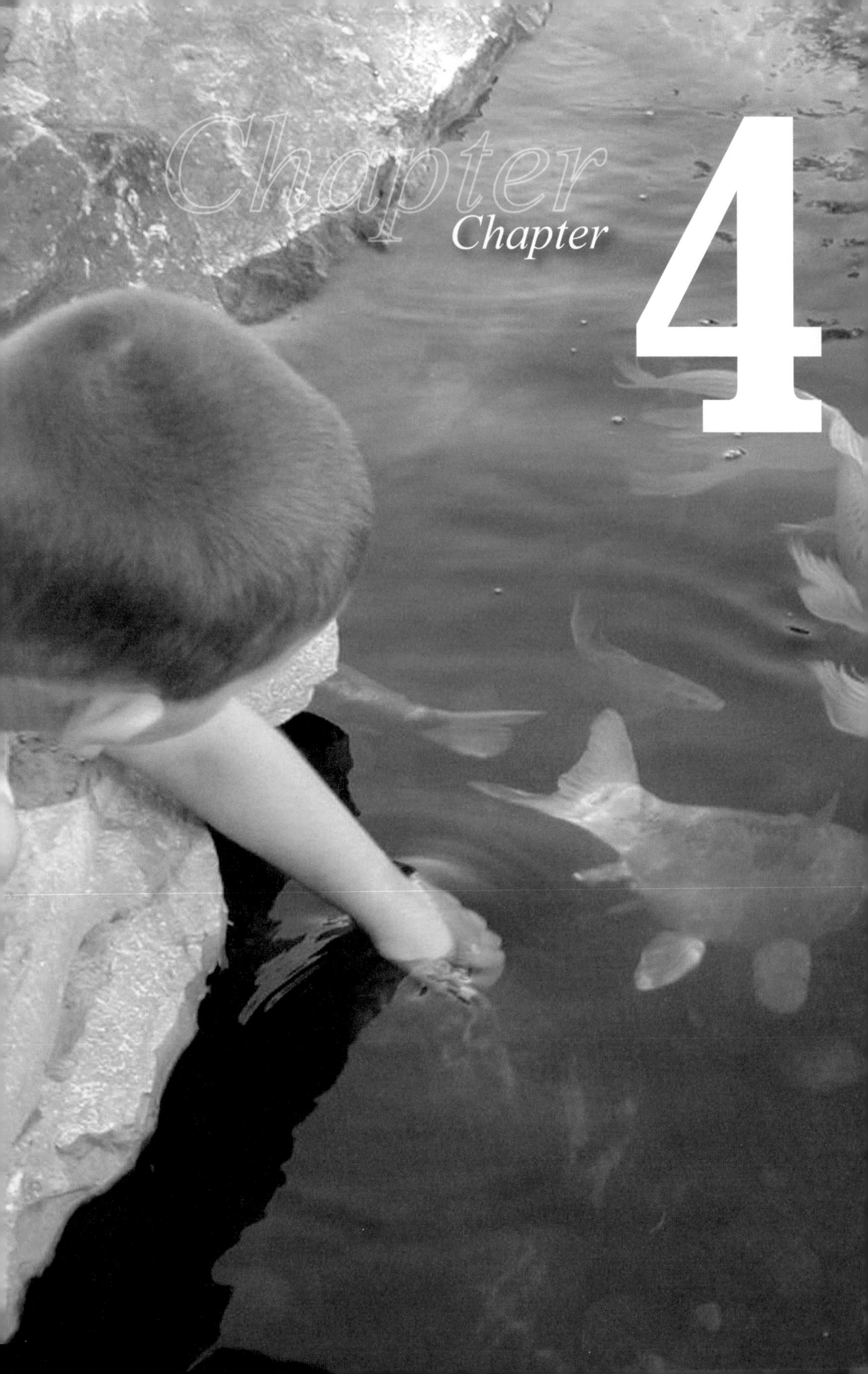

Chapter 4

Choosing Fish and Other Livestock

After all your plants are in place, wait a few weeks before adding fish to your pond. (A month is best.) That way, the oxygenators will have had a chance to root before the fish start feeding on them. It will also take that long for the water to warm up and release any harmful gases (most tap water contains chlorine [KLOR-een], which is toxic to fish). Don't worry if the algae is as thick as pea soup. Once the lilies are fully grown, the algae will die.

You don't really need fish for a water garden, but without a few of them to eat the insects, your pond will quickly seem like a mosquito-filled swamp.

How many fish should you buy? A deep pond supports no more fish than a shallow pond. What matters to the fish is the surface area. Think of the surface as your pond's lungs, breathing in oxygen and releasing carbon dioxide. A safe guideline is one fish for every 3 square feet of surface area. For our example pond of 50 square feet, you could have up to 16 fish. With this number, they will have plenty of room to grow and breed.

Goldfish are scavengers (SKAA-ven-jurs). They can help keep your pond clean.

Goldfish are the most popular pond fish. They are hardy, colorful, and inexpensive. If you follow the above stocking guideline, they will grow quite large.

Choose fish for their bright, solid colors. Spotted fish will blend into their surroundings. Almost any variety in the goldfish family will do well in your water garden. Koi and higoi carp require special filters, so you might want to avoid them.

Never put new fish directly into your pond. Keep them separate in a small aquarium for at least a week. That's about how long it will take for a sick fish to show symptoms or die.

It's a good idea to keep new fish in a fishbowl or aquarium (ah-KWAY-ree-um) for at least a week before you put them in your pond. In an aquarium, you can keep an eye on them for diseases. Big fish won't do well in a small aquarium, so it is better to buy young fish. When you know the fish are healthy, you can move them to the pond.

Don't pour fish directly into a pond or aquarium. They need time to adjust to the change in water temperature. Place them in a small container of the water they were in (such as a plastic bag), then set the container into the aquarium or pond. After about an hour, gently pour your fish into their new home. Don't feed them for the first two days.

To train your fish to "come to the table," tap the side of the pool. Then sprinkle a little food on the surface. Allow them five minutes to eat. If there's food left after five minutes, don't give them as much next time. If they eat it all quickly, give them a little more. Increase the amount of food regularly until they're full-grown. Use pellet or flaked food from a fish dealer, and vary their diet to keep them healthy.

Fish don't overeat, so you won't kill them by feeding them too much. However, uneaten food will decay and pollute the water. Feed your fish once a day at about the same time each day.

Don't put catfish or snails in your water garden. Catfish are scavengers, but they'll do more damage than good. Since goldfish are also scavengers, you don't need the catfish. Snails often hitchhike on plants, so check new plants carefully

Pond Tip

In the right conditions, goldfish can live for up to twenty years! The oldest known goldfish lived for forty-three years. Feed your fish a variety of foods and keep your pond clean. Don't put different types of fish in your pond either—stick to goldfish while you're learning.

Newts (left), toads, and even turtles may visit your pond. You might be tempted to catch them, but leave them alone. Just sit quietly and watch them enjoy your pond.

before planting. Don't panic if you miss one. A healthy pond can tolerate a few snails. They just aren't necessary, and they will compete with your fish for food. If you spot one and you don't want it in your pond, simply remove it.

Frogs, toads, turtles, and newts will also like your pond. They live both in water and on land. You can buy them, but there's no guarantee that they'll stick around. Most likely, wild ones will make your pond their new home. Newts eat fish fry. Usually, frogs don't hurt fish. In fact, your fish will eat the tadpoles, while the tadpoles will help keep the place clean (tadpoles are also scavengers).

You may lose some fish to a raccoon or hawk. The best protection is your pond's depth and its

Dragonflies are a common visitor to most ponds. When they rest, their wings are out to the sides. When damselflies rest, their wings point up.

The great diving beetle is a destructive guest. If you see one, use a net to remove it.

lilies. Your pond's plants and the flat rocks that hang over the inside edge of the pond (as described in chapter 3) will give your fish a place to hide from wild **predators**.

Your pond will attract dragonflies, damselflies, and even small beetles. However, the great diving beetle will kill your fish. These beetles are about 1½ inches long, and black with a narrow edge of brownish gold. They breathe air, so you can easily catch them with a net when they rise to the surface. Water boatmen also kill small fish. This beetle swims upside-down under the surface, using its hind legs like oars. Remove them with a net at once.

Maintenance and Troubleshooting

A balanced pond needs little upkeep. However, because it's a contained world, it will need some tender-loving care.

Perhaps the most drastic problem you could have is a leaking pond. If the concrete cracks or a liner tears, let the water level drop until it stops. The hole will be just above the water line. If the hole is in the bottom of the pond, all the water will leak out. Before it does, you'll need to move your fish to a temporary home. If your concrete pond has a crack, you'll need a professional to repair it. Most liners can be repaired with special kits.

A cracked pond or punctured liner might not be the problem. If you have a waterfall, turn off the pump. If the leaking stops, you'll know there's a leak in the waterfall's system. If it's a slow loss, just add water as needed and forget it. If you're losing inches a day, turn off the waterfall and have it repaired.

When it is sunny and dry for a long time, you may need to add water. Use a slow-trickling hose to top off the pond. If it's really rainy for a while, be careful of runoff water. It can be toxic if you use weed killer on your lawn.

A tear or hole in the lining must be repaired quickly to protect your plants and fish. Use a specially purchased repair kit, made for your lining type. Follow the directions exactly. Don't take shortcuts—they'll only make your work harder.

Once algae has invaded your pond, the water will never be as clear as tap water again. Healthy pond water is pale yellow or reddish brown. The key to an algae-free pond is balance and patience. Sometimes algae return in the spring. Once the lilies and oxygenators grow back, the algae will die.

A partial water change won't hurt your plants or fish if you do it correctly. Let the water trickle slowly into the pond to mix with the polluted water. Use a bucket or **siphon** (SY-fun) to remove up to a third of the pond's water as the new water replaces what you remove. The fish can remain in the pond, but replace the water slowly so that they can adjust to any temperature change in the water.

Decaying leaves and other **debris** (deh-BREE) will turn water black. Remove the debris and change one third of the water. To prevent the problem, cover your pond with netting during the fall to keep leaves from falling into the water. A dead fish can turn the water cloudy. Find the corpse, throw it away or bury it, and change up to one third of the water. Check your pond regularly for debris and dead fish to prevent water pollution.

If your lilies don't flower, the water may be too cold, the pond isn't getting enough sunlight, or you've planted the lilies too deeply. If **aphids** (AY-fids) attack them, do not use pesticides. Hose the aphids off into the water where the fish will eat them.

Pond Tip

Perhaps the best way to decide if you really want a water garden is to consider the potential for trouble. Most importantly, a pond, even a small one, can be dangerous to small children. If there is a toddler or preschooler around who might fall into the pond, you should probably wait to build your pond until the child is older. If you live in an area where there are wild alligators, check with your county extension office. They may advise you to skip a pond.

Examine your fish regularly. Move sick fish to a separate tank before they have a chance to spread their condition. Ick (pictured) is a common disease and easy to treat if you catch it early. Unfortunately, the white spots can be hard to see.

In the late summer, thin out the marginal plants, if necessary. When the oxygenators die in late summer, cut them back to just a few inches long. Also, remove dead leaves and blooms from your lilies.

Blanketweed can spread even for the most careful gardener. This simple plant forms long green threads. Twist a twig among the threads and pull them out.

In a healthy pond, a single fish can become infected with fungus. Usually, it happens after an injury. Move the infected fish to a separate tank, where you can treat it with medicine. If several fish become infected, it means your pond is polluted

Occasionally, you'll need to check all your pond's parts to make sure everything's working as it should. Add new plants in the spring and fall.

from too many fish or too much uneaten food. Change up to one third of the water. Then, reduce the number of fish or the amount of food.

During stormy weather, the pond cannot exchange carbon dioxide for oxygen. When this happens, the fish won't be able to breathe. If you don't have a waterfall, swish the surface of the water with a stick to release carbon dioxide.

Healthy fish in a healthy pond require almost no care other than food and an occasional water change. Polluted water is their number one enemy. Most sick fish die, so prevention is the key to their survival.

Craft
Toad House

You might not think of a toad as a regular visitor to a pond, but they do visit, and if you're lucky, you'll convince a few to stick around. They eat bugs! Just one toad can eat over 100 insects in a single day. Mostly, they eat at night—and that's when slugs and cutworms come out too. Left unchecked, slugs and cutworms can damage your pond's lining. Toads also eat beetles, so a toad is a good addition to a small pond or water garden. To make the area around your pond attractive to toads, you can make them a house.

What you'll need:

- A medium-sized clay or plastic flowerpot and saucer
- Waterproof paints (acrylics will work best)
- Paintbrushes
- Small hand spade
- Battery-operated night-light or solar light
- Dead leaves or mulch

What to do:

- If the pot's dirty, wash it and then set it out to dry completely.
- Use your paints and brushes to decorate it.
- Set the pot in a safe place to let the paint dry.
- Clean up your painting mess.
- Once the paint is thoroughly dry, lay the pot on its side near the edge of your pond.
- Bury the house about halfway into the ground.
- Place dead leaves or mulch on the "floor" of your toad house.
- Wait.

Toads don't use their mouths to drink. They sit in shallow water and soak water in through their skin. If your pond has a shallow end, the toads will sit there to drink. If not, place the saucer near the toad house and fill it with water. Place the light near the house. It will attract moths, which toads like to eat. With all these creature comforts, a few toads are bound to move in. Curious toads will move the mulch around, so you'll know if one's checking out the house. It should take only three or four days to get an interested toad. If nothing happens, move your house. You might have to try several places before the toads are happy with the location. Once a toad moves in, be sure to keep the saucer full of clean water, especially during hot weather. You can dip it right out of your pond!

Appendix 1: Math Formulas:
Surface Area, Volume, and Average Depth

Formula for figuring surface area

Shape	Formula	Example
rectangle	length x width	10 feet by 5 feet 10 x 5 = 50 square feet
square	length x width	7 feet square 7 x 7 = 49 square feet
circle	(diameter ÷ 2) x (diameter ÷ 2) x 3.142	10-foot circle 5 x 5 x 3.142 = 78.55 square feet
oval	(length x width) x 0.8	12 by 8 oval (12 x 8) x 0.8 = (96) x 0.8 = 76.8 square feet

Formula for figuring volume	Example
Surface area in square feet x average water depth in feet x 7.5	55 square feet by 24 inches 55 sq ft x 2 ft x 7.5 = 825 gallons

Formula for figuring average water depth	Example
Measure the depth at several different places throughout the pond, add them, then divide by the number of different depths taken. This will give you the depth.	Three measurements say 2 feet; three say 1 foot (2 + 2 + 2 + 1 + 1 + 1) ÷ 6 = 1.5 feet average depth

Appendix 2: Planting Water Lilies

Water lilies			
Planting Depth	Soil Depth*	Surface Coverage	Name (All in the genus *Nymphaea*)
3 to 9 inches	5 inches	1¼ square feet	*Pygmaea rubra* *Pygmaea alba* *Pygmaea helvola*
5 to 12 inches	7 inches	2 square feet	*Laydekeri lilacea* *Odorata minor*
7 to 15 inches	9 inches	3 square feet	*Laydekeri fulgens*
9 to 18 inches	9 inches	4 square feet	*Odorata sulphurea*
9 to 24 inches	9 inches	5 square feet	*Atropurpurea* *Odorata rosea* *Odorata alba*
12 to 30 inches	9 inches	6 square feet	*Marliacea carnea* *Marliacea albida* *Marliacea chromatella*
15 to 36 inches	9 inches	8 square feet	*Tuberosa rosea* *Alba* *Tuberosa richardsoni*

* Soil depth is the amount of soil in the pot necessary for healthy root growth (not how far down you place the roots in the soil). It also includes a ½-inch to 1-inch layer of gravel or pebbles on top of the soil.

pond depth − (soil depth + planting depth) = height of planting platform

Further Reading

Books

Beneke, Jeff. *Sunset Garden Pools: Fountains & Waterfalls*. Menlo Park, California: Sunset Books, 2002.

Lang, Susan, and T. Jeff Williams. *Water Gardens*. Menlo Park, California: Sunset Books, 2004.

Macaulay, Kelley, and Bobbie Kalman. *Goldfish* (Pet Care). New York: Crabtree Publishing Company, 2004.

Ostrow, Marshall E. *Goldfish* (Complete Pet Owner's Manual). New York: Barron's Educational Series, 2003.

Works Consulted

Archer-Wills, Anthony. *The Water Gardener*. New York: Barron's Education Series, Inc., 1993.

Dubé, Richard L. *Natural Pattern Forms: A Practical Sourcebook for Landscape Design*. New York: Van Nostrand Reinhold, 1997.

Heritage, Bill. *Ponds and Water Gardens*. London: Blandford Press, 1986.

Ledbetter, Gordon T. *The Book of Patios and Ponds*. Sherborne, England: Alphabooks, 1984.

Littlewood, Michael. *Landscape Detailing*. Oxford, Massachusetts: Architectural Press, 2001.

Robinson, Peter. *Water Gardens in a Weekend*. New York: Sterling Publishing Co., Inc., 2001.

Sawano, Takashi. *Creating Your Own Japanese Garden*. Tokyo, Japan: Shufunotomo Co., Ltd., 1999.

Seike, Kiyoshi, Masanobu Kudo, and David H. Engel. *A Japanese Touch for Your Garden*. New York: Kodansha International Ltd., 1980.

Slawson, David A. *Secret Teachings in the Art of Japanese Gardens*. New York: Kodansha International Ltd., 1987.

Sprin, Anne Whiston. *The Granite Garden: Urban Nature and Human Design*. New York: Basic Books, Inc., Publishers, 1985.

Swindells, Philip, and David Mason. *The Complete Book of the Water Garden*. Woodstock, New York: The Overlook Press, 1990.

Van Sweden, James. *Gardening with Water*. New York: Random House, 1995.

Wijaya, Made. *Tropical Garden Design*. Boston: Periplus Editions, 1999.

On the Internet

Pond Zone
http://www.pondzone.com/

Create a Garden Pond for Wildlife
http://4hwildlifestewards.org/pdfs/pond.pdf

How to Build a Water Garden or Fish Pond
http://www.watergarden.com/pages/build_wg.html

Gardening Water Features
http://www.hgtv.com/hgtv/gl_design_water_features/article/0,1785,HGTV_3575_2644263,00.html

Fine Gardening Waterworks
    http://www.taunton.com/finegardening/design/articles/waterworks.
    aspx?nterms=74910
Fine Gardening; Make a Big Splash With a Tiny Garden
    http://www.taunton.com/finegardening/design/articles/make-big-splash-
    with-tiny-water-garden.aspx?nterms=74910
DoItYourself.com; Wash Tub Water Garden;
    http://doityourself.com/stry/thewatergarden

Glossary

algae (AL-gee)—Tiny plants that live in water and can quickly cover the water's surface, harming the fish that live there.

aphid (AY-fid)—A tiny soft-bodied insect that feeds on the liquid in plant stems.

bog (BOG)—Wet, spongy ground.

compact (kom-PAKT)—Press firmly together.

debris (deh-BREE)—Tiny pieces of dead plant and animal matter.

ecosystem (EK-oh-sis-tum)—The plants and animals that live in an area with one another.

electrocute (ee-LEK-troh-kyoot)—To kill or injure with electricity.

fry (FRY)—Newborn fish.

nourish (NUR-ish)—Provide with food; help grow.

nutrients (NOO-tree-unts)—Chemicals that help things grow.

oxygenators (OK-seh-jeh-nay-turs)—Small plants that live below the water's surface and produce oxygen, which stays in the water for fish to breathe.

pesticide (PES-tih-syd)—A chemical that kills plant, animal, or insect pests.

predator (PREH-dih-ter)—An animal that feeds on other animals.

rhizome (RY-zohm)—A bark-like root.

scavengers (SKAA-ven-jurs)—Animals that feed on dead plant and animal matter.

siphon (SY-fun)—A hose that you fill with water and use to drain a container of water.

submersible (sub-MER-suh-bul)—Something that can be kept underwater.

surge (SURJ)—A sudden and strong wave of rushing water.

toxic (TOK-sik)—Poisonous.

algae 8, 24, 29, 38
aphids 39
beetles 24, 35, 44
birds 4, 9,
blanketweed 40
bogs 8
butyl rubber 13
carbon dioxide 8, 29, 41
concrete 13, 37
damselflies 34, 35
dragonflies 34, 35
ecosystem 7
electricity 18
fertilizer 24
fish 8, 11, 13, 19, 26, 29, 31, 32–
    35, 39, 40–41
    catfish 33
    goldfish 10, 30, 33
    higoi 30
    koi 10, 30
frogs 34
fry 26, 34
great diving beetle 35
grubs 24
heating element 8
lighting 14, 18, 21, 39, 44, 45
marginals (plants) 26–27, 40
mosquitoes 29
newts 33, 34
oxygen 8, 26, 29, 41
oxygenators (plants) 21, 25–26,
    29, 38, 40
pesticides 24, 37, 39
planting depth 17, 18, 21–23
plants 11, 13, 17, 18, 21–27, 41
    (and see water hyacinths,
    water lilies)
polythene 14, 15

polyvinyl chloride (PVC) 13–14,
    21
pond
    constructing 13–19
    dangers of 39
    depth of 7, 11, 14–15, 21–22,
        35, 42, 43
    design of 7–11, 17, 18, 19
    digging tips 16, 17, 18
    filling 8, 13, 17, 18, 19
    liners for 14–15, 17, 19, 23,
        37, 38
    location of 7–9, 11, 16
    materials for 13–14, 15, 16
    shape of 10, 11, 14, 15, 17, 42
    surface area of 9, 11, 26, 29,
        42
    visitors to 33–35, 42–43
    volume of 7, 11, 42
    water for 19, 37, 38–39
pumps 9, 25, 37
rhizomes 25
rocks, decorative 14, 19, 35
snails 33–34
surges 8
tadpoles 34
toads 33, 34, 42–43
turtles 34
water boatmen 35
waterfalls 4, 9, 34, 37, 41
water hyacinths 22
water lilies 8, 11, 21–25, 29, 35,
    38, 39, 40

PHOTO CREDITS: Cover, pp. 6, 27—Susan Sales Harkins and William H. Harkins; pp. 1, 10, 12, 20, 21, 24, 30, 31, 32—Jupiter Images; pp. 11, 14, 16, 17—Lauren Unsihuay; pp. 15, 19—Faith Rowland; pp. 22, 41—Barbara Marvis